Only
Believe

GARLAND JONES
DR. KEVIN B. LEE

Only Believe
Copyright @ 2016 Garland Jones

Publisher's Cataloging-in-Publication Data

International Standard Book Number: 978-1-51427-782-9 (trade paperback)

Published in the United States of America

Contact Garland Jones: Telephone: (866) 535-7997

Contact Dr. Kevin Lee: Telephone: (678) 240-2213

This journal/book is dedicated to
people who want to
ONLY BELIEVE

TABLE OF CONTENTS

Definitions

Introduction   2

Believe the Impossible   8
God is Able   17
Ask and Receive   27
Don't Be Afraid   37
Power to Believe   47
See and Believe   57
Christ Gives Strength   67
Why Me?   77
Being Confident   87
Trusting in God   97
Listening to God   107
Believe and Don't Doubt   117
Who Do You Trust?   127
Joy and Peace   137
Only Believe   147

About the Authors   160

only

adverb

adverb: **only**

and no one or nothing more besides; solely or exclusively:

synonyms: exclusively · solely · to the exclusion of everything else

no more than (implying that more was hoped for or expected); merely:

synonyms: merely · simply · just

adjective

adjective: **only**

alone of its or their kind; single or solitary:

synonyms: sole · single · one (and only) · solitary · lone · unique · exclusive

believe

accept (something) as true; feel sure of the truth
of:
synonyms: regard as true · accept · be convinced
by · give credence to ·
credit · trust · put confidence in · swallow · buy ·
go for hold (something) as an opinion; think or
suppose:

INTRODUCTION

I believe God has a purpose for our lives.

Believe in God's purpose for your life. Everyone was born with a purpose.

That is why you are here.

Never underestimate what God really wants to do in your life and the destiny He has written for you.

Throughout my life, my parents have continued to remind me that before I was born they asked God to give them wisdom on how to raise, mold and guide me into the person God wanted me to be not what they wanted me to be. They have prayed this every day since I was in my mom's belly. My dad would talk to me through my mom's belly speaking great things into my life and making sure that I knew his voice. When my dad would say "It's your Daddy" I would start moving and kicking with excitement. When I was born my parents tell me I immediately knew my dad's voice.

God is our Heavenly Father and He desires that we ONLY BELIEVE in Him, His Word and His plan for our lives. When you spend time in His Word and talking with Him you begin to recognize His voice more and more each day.

Just like I recognized my natural father's voice when I was born because he talked to me every day while I was in the womb, the same is for God. God's Word is His voice and the truth. If we spend time in the Word and praying, God will speak to us audibly. You will know it's our Heavenly Father.

BELIEVE is a powerful word. If you look at the definition at the beginning of the book – Believe means to accept something as true, to place confidence in completely.

People tend to think they are not qualified to do something, but nothing is impossible with God! Believe in God and His plan for you. He uses every life experience to fulfill His destiny for you if you let Him.

Remember you will have obstacles, temptations adversities, and situations that are designed to stop you from fulfilling God's plan for your life. Their job is to try to cause confusion and doubt in hopes of taking you down and destroying your present and future. Through each blow, swing, dagger and jab you have to stay on track and continue to move forward – focusing on Jesus and believing in God.

My belief in God and the Word of God has strongly influenced the way I think, make decisions and how I look at life. My belief in God and His Word has influenced my decisions, my goals, my behaviour and my relationships with other people.

Trust God. Let God lead you in the right direction. Don't try to create your own plan for your life. God's plan is better than yours. Don't try to do things your way.

Take a moment and think about the following questions:

How do you look at your life?

Who or what influences your life?

Who or what influences your decisions?

Who or what influences your goals?

Who or what influences your behaviour?

Who or what influences your relationship with others?

The Word of God is what I base everything on in my life.

I believe that in spite of any family issues or history we all have the opportunity to be the "maverick" of our family. With God we can overcome generational obstacles and problems and become who God wants us to become.

Passion and courage are components of a great legacy to pass on from generation to generation. Don't give up. Don't quit. Don't let people or things distract you from your destiny. That is what separates people who make an impact during their lifetime from those who just exist on the earth.

Leave a Godly heritage. That is worth more than ANYTHING else.

The more you take bold steps towards achieving your destiny, the more you push beyond the limits, the more you discover your capabilities, the more courageous and confident you become. The more God opens doors.

God does not want us to be afraid with the gifts He has given us. We are to be bold, loving, and disciplined.

This is a journal to challenge you to seek God first. There are different scripture references and reflective questions on every ten pages throughout this journal. You can choose any one of them to read, meditate on and/or answer the questions in your own order. You may want to start with one of the scriptures in the middle, end or beginning. It is up to you.

Ask God what is His plan and destiny for your life. Write down any thoughts and/or prayer requests. Write down the vision God gives you for your life. Answer the questions honestly. Spend some quiet time with God. Open up before God and don't keep anything back. God will do what needs to be done and make His plans for your life clear if you commit everything to Him. Write down how God is moving in your life. He is for you always. God is right here with you. Trust God. He made you and He knows His will for your life.

ONLY BELIEVE! – Garland Jones

CHAPTER 1
Believe the Impossible

"If you can?" said Jesus. "Everything is possible
for one who believes." Mark 9:23 NIV

Please journal your thoughts on the following questions

What keeps you from believing the impossible?

What is God stretching you to believe?

_____

_____

_____

_____

_____

_____

_____

_____

_____

_____

_____

_____

What has God done because of your belief in Him?

_____

_____

_____

_____

_____

_____

_____

_____

_____

_____

_____

_____

What does it mean to believe in God?

_____

_____

_____

_____

_____

_____

_____

_____

_____

_____

_____

_____

_____

_____

CHAPTER 2
<u>God is Able</u>

Now glory be to God, who by his mighty
power at work within us is able to do far more
than we would ever dare to ask or even dream
of – infinitely beyond our highest prayers,
desires, thoughts or hopes.
Ephesians 3:20 TLB
Please journal your thoughts on the following questions

What's your greatest dream?

What are some things you have considered doing?

_____

_____

_____

_____

_____

_____

_____

_____

_____

_____

_____

What do you dare to believe?

How are you radical in what you believe?

_____

_____

_____

_____

_____

_____

_____

_____

_____

_____

_____

_____

CHAPTER 3
<u>Ask and Receive</u>

**And whatever you ask for in prayer, believing,
you will receive. Matthew 21:22 AMP**
Please journal your thoughts on the following questions

What are some things you are asking for?

_____

_____

_____

_____

_____

_____

_____

_____

_____

What are some things you have asked for in the past and have received? How did it make you feel?

_____

_____

_____

_____

_____

_____

_____

_____

_____

_____

_____

_____

What are some things you have asked for but have not received?

_____

_____

_____

_____

_____

_____

_____

_____

_____

_____

_____

_____

33

What are some things you desire but have not
asked for?

_____

_____

_____

_____

_____

_____

_____

_____

_____

_____

_____

_____

CHAPTER 4
Don't Be Afraid

Hearing this, Jesus said to Jairus, "Don't be afraid; just believe, and she will be healed."
Luke 8:50 NIV
Please journal your thoughts on the following questions

What brings you the most fear?

_____

_____

_____

_____

_____

_____

_____

_____

What fears hinder your belief?

_____

_____

_____

_____

_____

_____

_____

_____

_____

_____

_____

_____

_____

How do your fears hinder your belief?

_____

_____

_____

_____

_____

_____

_____

_____

_____

_____

_____

_____

_____

How does your belief affect your fears?

CHAPTER 5
<u>Power to Believe</u>

Therefore I tell you, whatever you ask for in prayer, believe that you have received it, and it will be yours. Mark 11:24 NIV

Please journal your thoughts on the following questions

What are you believing God for?

_____

_____

_____

_____

_____

_____

_____

_____

_____

How are you activating your faith?

_____

_____

_____

_____

_____

_____

_____

_____

_____

_____

_____

_____

_____

What type of lifestyle do you live that hinders
your prayers from being answered?

_____

_____

_____

_____

_____

_____

_____

_____

_____

_____

_____

What type of lifestyle do you live that helps your prayers become answered?

_____

_____

_____

_____

_____

_____

_____

_____

_____

_____

_____

_____

CHAPTER 6
<u>See and Believe</u>

"But didn't I tell you that you will see a
wonderful miracle from God if you believe?"
Jesus asked her.
John 11:40 TLB

Please journal your thoughts on the following questions

What is a miracle? DO you believe in miracles?

_____

_____

_____

_____

_____

_____

_____

_____

Can you remember a time God created a miracle
for you or someone else?

_____

_____

_____

_____

_____

_____

_____

_____

_____

_____

_____

_____

_____

List some miracles in the bible

_____

_____

_____

_____

_____

_____

_____

_____

_____

_____

_____

How do other people's miracles influence what you believe?

CHAPTER 7
<u>Christ Gives Strength</u>

For I can do everything through Christ, who gives me strength. Philippians 4:13 NLT
Please journal your thoughts on the following questions

What do you need strength for?

_____

_____

_____

_____

_____

_____

_____

_____

_____

Can your strength become depleted? How?

_____

_____

_____

_____

_____

_____

_____

_____

_____

_____

_____

_____

_____

What depletes your strength in Christ?

_____

_____

_____

_____

_____

_____

_____

_____

_____

_____

_____

_____

How do you maintain your strength in Christ?

CHAPTER 8
Why Me?

For we are God's masterpiece. He has created
us anew in Christ Jesus, so we can do the good
things he planned for us long ago.
Ephesians 2:10 NLT

Please journal your thoughts on the following questions

What is a masterpiece?

_____

_____

_____

_____

_____

_____

_____

_____

Do you see yourself as one of God's masterpieces?
How?

_____

_____

_____

_____

_____

_____

_____

_____

_____

_____

_____

_____

How is God using you as a masterpiece for the good of your family?

_____

_____

_____

_____

_____

_____

_____

_____

_____

_____

_____

How is God using you as a masterpiece for the good of those you hang around?

CHAPTER 9
<u>Being Confident</u>

**Being confident of this, that He who began a
good work in you will carry it on to
completion until the day of Christ Jesus.
Philippians 1:6 NIV**

Please journal your thoughts on the following questions

What does confidence mean?

_____

_____

_____

_____

_____

_____

_____

Where is your confidence in God on a scale of 1-10 (with 10) being the highest?

How do you allow God to help you?

_____

_____

_____

_____

_____

_____

_____

_____

_____

_____

_____

_____

What is God trying to get you to complete/finish?

CHAPTER 10
<u>Trusting in God</u>

**Trust in and rely confidently on the Lord with
all your heart and do not rely on your own
insight or understanding Proverbs 3:5 AMP**
Please journal your thoughts on the following questions

What does the word trust mean?

What does the word confidence mean?

When have you trusted God with all your heart?

_____

_____

_____

_____

_____

_____

_____

_____

_____

_____

_____

_____

What keeps you from trusting God? Why?

CHAPTER 11
Listening to God

Listen to God's voice in everything you do and everywhere you go; He's the one who will keep you on track. Proverbs 3:6 MSG ·

Please journal your thoughts on the following questions

Can you recognize God's voice?

_____

_____

_____

_____

_____

_____

_____

_____

_____

How do you recognize God voice?

_____

_____

_____

_____

_____

_____

_____

_____

_____

_____

_____

How do we miss God's voice?

_____

_____

_____

_____

_____

_____

_____

_____

_____

_____

_____

_____

_____

Is there a difference in hearing God and listening to God?

CHAPTER 12
<u>Believe and Don't Doubt</u>

But when you ask, you must believe and not
doubt, because the one who doubts is like a
wave of the sea, blown and tossed by the wind.
James 1:6 NIV

Please journal your thoughts on the following questions

How does your faith waver?

_____

_____

_____

_____

_____

_____

_____

_____

How is your faith strong?

How does your faith push you through your trials?

_____

_____

_____

_____

_____

_____

_____

_____

_____

_____

_____

Share a time when faith overcame your doubt?

_____

_____

_____

_____

_____

_____

_____

_____

_____

_____

_____

_____

CHAPTER 13
Who Do You Trust?

It is better to trust the Lord than put
confidence in men.
Psalms 118:8 TLB
Please journal your thoughts on the following questions

Who do you trust the most? Why?

_____

_____

_____

_____

_____

_____

_____

_____

_____

Why is it important to trust?

Can you trust the wrong person?

What's the difference between trusting God and
man?

_____

_____

_____

_____

_____

_____

_____

_____

_____

_____

_____

_____

_____

136

CHAPTER 14
Joy and Peace

May the God of hope fill you with joy and peace in believing [through the experience of your faith] that by the power of the Holy Spirit you will abound in hope and overflow with confidence in His promises.
Romans 15:13 AMP

Please journal your thoughts on the following questions

Where do you get your joy and peace from?

_____

_____

_____

_____

_____

_____

_____

How do you receive joy and peace?

How does confidence in God's Word bring joy?

_____
_____
_____
_____
_____
_____
_____
_____
_____
_____
_____
_____
_____
_____

How does confidence in God's Word bring peace?

CHAPTER 15
Only Believe

But overhearing what they said, Jesus said to the ruler of the synagogue, "Do not fear; only believe." Mark 5:36 ESV

Please journal your thoughts on the following questions

Whose words have power over your life?

_____

_____

_____

_____

_____

_____

_____

_____

_____

What impact does God's word have on your life?

_____

_____

_____

_____

_____

_____

_____

_____

_____

_____

_____

_____

How does the Words of Jesus impact your life?

_____

_____

_____

_____

_____

_____

_____

_____

_____

_____

_____

_____

_____

ONLY BELIEVE

About the Authors

Garland loves God. He is a young man on a mission. Garland is a motivational speaker, author, business owner, director, producer, actor and athlete. Garland has a passion to teach and inspire his generation and beyond to believe and trust God with all of their hearts and seek Him first for the true destiny for their lives.

Garland is the founder of the 923Believe Company that promotes bold and trendy merchandise for everyone who chooses to believe.

Garland is currently pursuing his Bachelor Degree in Ministry and Master's Degree in Counseling. He is a New York Film Academy (NYFA) Graduate and a member of the Georgia's 21st Century Leader 20 under 20 Class of 2013 and Inaugural Recipient of the Turner Voices Award.

About the Authors

Kevin B. Lee is the Senior Pastor of Berean Christian Church in Snellville, Georgia. He has served in youth ministry for over 20 years. Dr. Lee earned a Doctorate of Ministry degree from United Theological Seminary in Dayton, Ohio. He received a Master's of Religious Education and a Master's of Divinity from Southwestern Theological Seminary in Fort Worth, Texas. He obtained a Bachelor of Arts degree in Criminal Justice from Langston University in Langston, Oklahoma.

Dr. Kevin B. Lee is the Founder of KBL Ministries. He has authored four books: Putting the Pieces Together, Making the Pieces Fit, Teaching Pieces to the Puzzle and Practical Pieces to the Puzzle, all geared towards youth ministry.

Dr. Lee has been married over 30 years and has two children and two grandchildren.

CONTACT THE AUTHORS

Contact Garland Jones

Email: 923believe@gmail.com

www.facebook.com/923Believe

Telephone: (866) 535-7997

Contact Dr. Kevin B. Lee

www.kbleeministries.org

www.bereangwinnett.org

www.buildingasolidyouthministry.org

Follow Dr. Lee on:

Instagram and Twitter: pkleeministries

Telephone: (678) 240-2213

Made in the USA
San Bernardino, CA
26 February 2017